Just Hanging Around

Who do you know
that swings through the trees,
hanging upside down
with the greatest of ease?

3

Did You Know...

Most monkeys can climb trees. Some monkeys use their tail like an extra hand to hold on to branches.

A monkey.

Who do you know
that roosts by day,
sleeping upside down
while others play?

7

Did You Know...

Bats are the only mammals able to fly. Bats hunt at night. Most bats eat insects. Without bats, many crops would be ruined.

A bat.

Who do you know
that moves so very slow,
clinging upside down
to trees as it goes?

11

Did You Know...

Sloths spend most of their lives hanging upside down in trees. A sloth can take a full day to move from one tree to another.

A sloth.

Who do you know
that has a knack
for swimming upside down
to catch a snack?

14

15

Did You Know...

The upside-down catfish swims belly-up. It looks for food under leaves in the water.

A catfish.

Who do you know
that sings for hours,
flipping upside down
to sip nectar from flowers?

19

Did You Know...

New Zealand tuis are forest songbirds. They use their long beak and tongue to get nectar from flowers.

A tui.

Who do you know
that can jump, play, and run,
hanging upside down
on the bars for fun?

23

Children!